Stage 1

TopReaders

By the Shore

Denise Ryan

Contents

Let's go down to the shore
and see what we can find!

On the Shore

Shores are where oceans
and seas meet the land.

cliff

Some shores have cliffs and
sandy beaches.

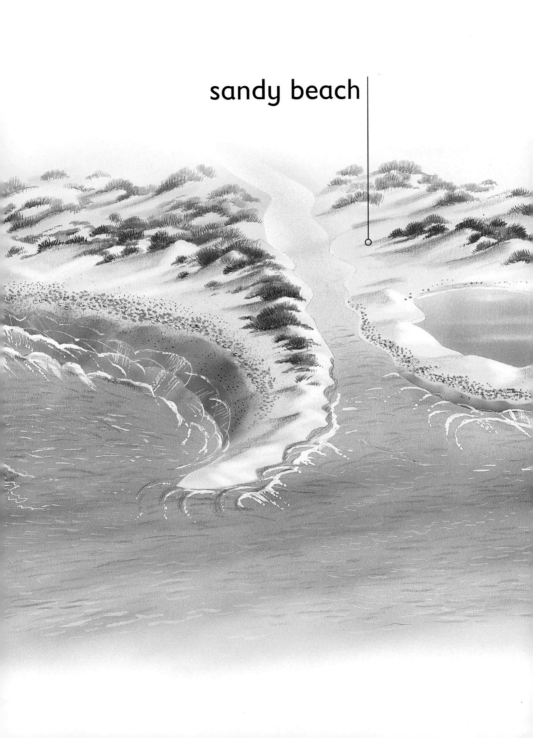

sandy beach

Whale Watching

Whales sometimes swim along the shore as they move from place to place.

whales

People watch whales from the cliffs.

Shore Birds

Some birds make their homes near sandy shores and rocky cliffs.

skimmer

pelican

Shore birds are good swimmers. Many have webbed feet.

puffin

webbed foot

booby

webbed foot

Dinner Time

Sea birds look for fish and insects near the shore.

terns

Some sea birds fight each other for their dinner.

shearwaters

cormorants

Shore Plants

Tough plants grow
in the sand. They stop
the sand from
blowing away.

pigface

Only small plants can grow
on sandy shores.

banksia

spinifex

At the Beach

People enjoy playing games at the beach.

These people are playing
a game of beach volleyball.

Sea Shells

You can find all kinds of sea shells on the shore.

whelk

sea urchin

oyster

scallop

Tiny animals live inside sea shells. The shells keep them safe.

sea star

cowrie

periwinkle

mussel

clam

Look Down!

Different kinds of plants
and animals live together
in rock pools.

Fish, sea otters, and sea urchins
live in this rock pool.

fish

sea otter

sea
urchins

Mangrove Forests

Mangrove forests are safe places for fish, birds, crabs, and shellfish.

mangrove

ghost nipper

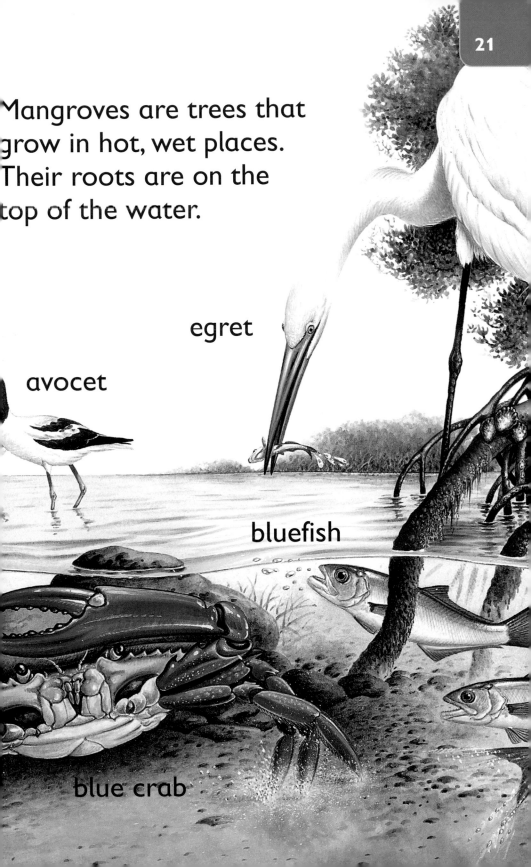

Mangroves are trees that grow in hot, wet places. Their roots are on the top of the water.

egret

avocet

bluefish

blue crab

City Shore

Many birds live near the city's lake shore.

mockingbird

falcon

People feed the birds near the shore.

pigeons

Quiz

Can you match each creature with its name?

pelican   pigeon

mussel   sea star